ALL THINGS TIGERS FOR KIDS

FILLED WITH PLENTY OF FACTS, PHOTOS, AND FUN TO LEARN ALL ABOUT TIGERS

ANIMAL READS

WWW.ANIMALREADS.COM

THIS BOOK BELONGS TO...

_____

_____

WWW.ANIMALREADS.COM

CONTENTS

Big Cats in Striped Pajamas	1
What Is A Tiger?	5
Let's Meet Different Types of Tigers!	17
Where Did Tigers Come From?	37
Characteristics and Appearance	45
What Do Tigers Eat?	57
Tiger Circle of Life	61
Quirky Facts You Probably Didn't Know About Tigers!	65
Did You Have Fun Learning About Tigers?	71
Thank You!	77

BIG CATS IN STRIPED PAJAMAS

Did you know that the terrific tiger is the largest cat in the world? It's pretty crazy, considering you might have a tiny tiger roaming around your house while you sleep.

YES, cats are indeed related to tigers!

Even if you don't have one of your own, we bet you probably still know a great deal about cats.

The roaming at night? Yep, that's a trait that tigers and cats share. Yet, even though these two awesome animals do share a few similarities, they really are worlds apart.

Eager to know more about this huge, roaring cat?

Then join us as we dive into the wild and wonderful world of tigers, one of the most awe-inspiring (and even a little bit scary) animals in the world.

Let's go!

HOW DO TIGERS DESCRIBE THEMSELVES?

PURR-fect!

WHAT IS A TIGER?

The mighty tiger, whose scientific name is *Panthera Tigris*, is part of the cat family of animals called *Felidae*. Ever heard of the term *'feline'*?

Well, that's where the word comes from! Feline means to be cat-like!

Anyway, the Felidae family includes a **LOT** of big cats. Cheetahs, lions, jaguars, leopards, and pumas are all examples of Felidae family members. And, you know what? So is the typical domestic house cat!

Tigers are the largest member of the cat family and can grow to a truly impressive size. They can weigh up to 700 pounds (**that's the weight of six adult humans combined!**), up to 12.5 feet in length (**slightly shorter than a family car!**), and up to about 3.5 feet tall.

Does it surprise you to know that tigers are bigger than lions? Seems strange, right? But lions have puffy hairdos that make them look bigger than they are, and in reality, they are taller than tigers but not nearly as chunky!

<u>**Fun Fact:**</u> The largest tiger ever recorded was Jaipur, a gorgeous kitty held in captivity. This Siberian tiger weighed a massive 900 pounds

and measured almost 11 feet, nose to tail-tip. *Wonder what they fed him?!*

Tigers have been studied by experts for more than 200 years. What they noted, most of all, is that this **BIG** cat was found all over the place – tigers have been found in Turkey and Russia, as well as China and on the foothills of the Himalayan Mountains in India. There were also tigers in Indonesia, on the islands of Bali and Java. Tigers sure did get around a lot! Thank goodness for such big paws...

So, how did tigers manage to travel far and wide? One reason experts give is that tigers, as opposed to other big cats like lions, prefer to live alone. This makes them **solitary animals.** They are not too social, and this need for space means they roamed a lot more. Traveling far means a tiger can be a little bit greedy with its food – it prefers not to share its meals, so it will always look out for remote places where there are no other tigers.

The only reason a tiger might stay with others is if there isn't enough hunting ground available to find their own place to live. Unfortunately, this is happening a lot more often nowadays, because many countries are chopping down their wild forests, which is very sad indeed.

Tigers are known as **apex (or top) predators** and **carnivores**, which means they are right at the top of the food chain on our planet. They hunt other animals for food but are not themselves hunted by other animals. Well, except humans, unfortunately.

Everything about a tiger makes them perfect hunters.

They are large and strong, fast runners, and have long sharp claws for grabbing their prey and not letting go.

As much as we'd all love to hug a tiger, or at least pet one, it probably isn't a very good idea. While tigers don't usually attack people, they are still different from your lovable goofy cat, who has much smaller teeth and claws.

FUN FACT: Cats and tigers share 96.5% of their DNA, which means they are almost identical. However, the 3.5% difference makes a massive difference!

Another thing big about tigers is their teeth. *Do you know their teeth grow up to four inches long?!* That's about the length from the base of your thumb to the tip of your pointer finger. Good thing tigers don't need to brush their teeth. **They would need a ton of toothpaste!**

One reason tigers don't have to brush their teeth is because they stay away from candy and sugary sodas. This makes them *very smart cats* too. But there is also another reason. Just like dogs, tigers chew on bones. Chewing on bones actually keeps their teeth clean. As predators and carnivores, tigers eat meat with plenty of bones. Tigers aren't picky about the kind of meat they eat, just as long as there is a lot of it! They have a big appetite, and they happily eat animals like wild boar, deer, and even small elephants!

Can you imagine eating an elephant? We know we can't. But tigers are up for the job.

Just point them to the nearest all-you-can-eat animal buffet!

HEY, KITTY, WHAT'S WITH THE STRIPED PAJAMAS?!

Aside from their humongous size, the most distinctive aspect of tigers is their beautiful striped coat. Other wild cats like jaguars, leopards, and cheetahs have spots, but the tiger is the only big cat with stripes.

So, are they really pajamas? Are they just there *to look fun*? Apparently, not!

As it happens, every tiger has a unique stripe pattern. That's right, no two tigers in the world have the exact same markings! Just like us humans are unique, a tiger's pattern is their very own personal, unique design. That means if you ever decide to study tigers someday in the wild, you would be able to tell them apart just by memorizing their special stripes.

Another animal with unique stripes is the zebra, but sticking zebras in a tiger book might not be too smart or safe (*especially for the zebras*). We think they'll have to have their own book, don't you?!

LET'S MEET DIFFERENT TYPES OF TIGERS!

Y ou might be surprised to learn there are actually nine different kinds of tigers, called *subspecies*. Sadly, three subspecies of tigers are now **extinct**, which means there are no more of these beautiful animals left anywhere on earth.

This also means there are six kinds of tigers around today.

Are you ready to dive in and learn all about these groups?

Let's explore them one by one!

SIBERIAN TIGER (*PANTHERA TIGRIS ALTAICA*)

If you've seen or read *The Jungle Book,* you might think tigers only live in jungles in India. But that isn't true! Did you know tigers also live in the snowy forests of Russia? This special cat does precisely this!

The Siberian tiger (also known as the Amur tiger) is the biggest member of the tiger family. A male Siberian tiger can grow as long as 10.5 feet in length or longer. That means if he stood on his toes, he would be taller than a basketball hoop.

How cool would it be to have a Siberian tiger on your basketball team?!

Siberian tigers are also the heaviest tigers, weighing as much as 660 pounds. That's the weight of about 60 bowling balls combined! Females are a bit smaller and can grow up to 8.5 feet long and weigh 370 pounds.

What makes the Siberian tiger unusual in the world of tigers is its pale orange fur and brown stripes. This is different from the bright orange and black stripe combination that you're used to on other tigers. They also have white on their chest and bellies, along with white around their necks. It's as if they're wearing a necklace!

Almost 100 years ago, only about 35 Siberian tigers were left in its natural region, which stretched the far east of Russia and northeast China. People cut down too much wild forest, and tiger numbers dramatically reduced. Thanks to major conservation efforts in the area, however, there are now around 350 tigers today, which is super great news!

Since tigers need forest (*and plenty of wild forest animals to hunt*), the area is now heavily protected. While Siberian tigers have a long way to go to bring their numbers up, some zoos have started trying to breed more Siberian tigers to help their cause. Let's hope this amazing kind of tiger can make a comeback and be around for many years to come.

FUN FACT: *The Siberian is the only tiger species that lives and can survive in the snow. That's one tough kitty!*

BENGAL OR INDIAN TIGER (*PANTHERA TIGRIS TIGRIS*)

If you go to the lake, do you usually take your cat? Probably not! Most cats don't love to swim.

In fact, they hate getting wet. But Bengal tigers, also known as Indian tigers, absolutely love to swim!

Out of all tigers, the Bengal tiger has the highest numbers still living in the wild. These tigers can be found throughout parts of India, Bhutan, Bangladesh, and Nepal. However, even though India has the most tigers of any area of the world — *there are only 2,500 to 3,750 Bengals in total* — the Bengal tigers are still considered endangered.

The wild tigers of India mostly spend time in dry and wet forests and grasslands. This stunning cat also has a pretty big secret: they can come out with white fur! Have you ever seen a white Bengal tiger? They look so cool!

Now, while this is indeed very cool, being born with white fur is actually a disadvantage to a Bengal. This means life is more difficult for them.

Why?

Because tigers hunt at night, and the dark fur helps them hide in tall grass. So, while a white tiger is beautiful, it stands out far too much at night, and so a white tiger is not such a successful hunter, after all.

FUN FACT: *The Bengal has the largest canine tooth of all the big cats and can chow down up to 90 pounds of meat in just a single meal. After that, the Bengal falls into a food coma and can go three whole weeks without eating!*

SOUTH CHINA TIGER (*PANTHERA TIGRIS AMOYENSIS*)

The South China tiger can be found in (*can you guess it?*)... **China**! They are one of the smallest tiger species, and sadly, there are only around 47 South China tigers left in the world. All of them now live in zoos and tiger sanctuaries throughout China.

Since there are so few of them, South China tigers are *almost* extinct. This is because a long time ago, they were hunted in the wild. Poachers would hunt these beautiful animals for their unique fur, which is bright yellow with broad stripes.

Now, we only know about 47 South China tigers. However, according to the **Save The Tigers Fund**, some wild South China tigers might still live in remote mountain ranges of three of the country's many provinces. We sure hope this is true! Wouldn't it be great to see these tigers make a comeback in the wild?

FUN FACT: Being smaller means the South China tiger is actually a speedy runner. It can run at a speed of 60 miles an hour, which is 20 miles an hour faster than the Siberian tiger! The tiger, overall, is the second-fastest big cat in the world. Do you know which one is the fastest? We'll give you a tip... it's the cheetah!

A cheetah sprinting almost too fast for the camera!

MALAYAN TIGER (*PANTHERA TIGRIS JACKSONI*)

The Malayan tiger is the newest member of the tiger family. It was only discovered as a different subspecies of tiger in 2004! It is almost identical to the Indo-Chinese tiger (*we'll tell you more about them later!*) and was only discovered to be different because scientists analyzed the DNA of different Indo-Chinese tigers and found some were not the same species!

Did you notice the end of the Malayan Tiger's scientific name, *"jacksoni?"* The new tiger subspecies was named after tiger conservationist

Peter Jackson, to honor his dedication and work with tigers.

So, who knows, if you decide to work with tigers someday, maybe a new tiger could be named after you!

The Malayan tiger is a smaller tiger found in the tropical forests of Malaysia and southern Thailand. Sadly, these tigers are also endangered, although the country of Malaysia is trying to protect them from hunters and trappers.

FUN FACT: Did you know these tigers actually help farmers? One of the Malayan tiger's favorite things to

eat is wild boar (a kind of wild pig with tusks). Boars can be a major pain for farmers as they cause a lot of damage to the crops they grow. While Malayan tigers may not wear overalls, plant seeds, or help weed the fields, they still help the farmers by hunting the wild boar that destroy their crops.

INDO-CHINESE TIGER (*PANTHERA TIGRIS CORBETTI*)

The Indo-Chinese tiger, which is nearly identical to the Malayan tiger, is also known as Corbett's tiger. It was named after Jim Corbett, a British tracker — another guy who got to have a tiger named after him!

The Indo-Chinese tiger is found in remote mountain areas throughout Laos, Thailand, Burma, Vietnam, and Cambodia. There are only thought to be 342 Corbett tigers still alive, so they are listed as endangered, which means their numbers are decreasing every year. Most of these tigers live in Thailand in tropical broadleaf forests.

The Indo-Chinese tiger has darker fur with narrower and shorter stripes than Bengals but are also a lot smaller. Mind you, a small tiger is still a *pretty big cat*! A male can measure up to nine feet long and weigh around 400 pounds. As usual, females are smaller, reaching around eight feet long and about 250 pounds. Can you imagine a 400-pound cat roaming around your kitchen? I think I'd feel a little nervous about that!

Have you ever felt shy, like you want to be all alone? If you have, then you know what it's like to be an Indo-Chinese tiger. These tigers live in mountainous forests and like to keep to themselves. If you went strolling through a tropical forest in Thailand or into the mountains, you might walk right past one of these quiet tigers watching you as it hid in the shadows.

Because they prefer to keep a low profile, we don't know much about how these tigers live in the wild. But we do know they are majestic animals that need our protection.

SUMATRAN TIGER (*PANTHERA TIGRIS SUMATRAE*)

The Sumatran tiger is only found on the island of Sumatra in Indonesia. Sumatran tigers live in large natural forests and don't do well out in the open in grasslands. Unfortunately, their forests keep getting cut down to build farms.

Without enough land to spread out and enough smaller animals to eat, these tigers are now endangered.

It's really sad that, despite the law to protect these tigers, they are still hunted for their fur and other parts. Hunters who kill protected animals, like Sumatran tigers, are called poachers. Poachers can pay big fines or go to jail for hunting endangered animals. However, sadly, many tigers are still hunted each year by poachers. It's important to know what's happening to the tigers, so we can try to help them and raise awareness that tigers need to be protected.

The Sumatran tiger has the darkest fur of all the tigers and twice as many large black stripes covering their body. They also have striped legs and are one of the smallest cats of the tiger family. The boys can grow eight feet long, but they will only weigh around 260 pounds. Girl Sumatran tigers can grow up to seven feet long and will weigh about 200 pounds. This is still a **BIG** cat, but a small, **BIG** cat.

<u>FUN FACT:</u> To help ensure the survival of the Sumatran tiger, the Indonesian Zoological Parks' Association has partnered with zoos throughout Indonesia, Australia, North America, and Europe to find them homes. This way, these tigers have a higher chance of survival and are safe from poachers. It would be better if they could live freely in their natural homes, but hopefully, this will become an option in the future.

HOW DO YOU TAKE A TIGER'S TEMPERATURE?

Very carefully!

WHERE DID TIGERS COME FROM?

The Javan tiger was a subspecies that is now extinct, but do you know that the place they lived, Java, is home to one of the oldest tiger fossils ever discovered? In case you didn't know, a *fossil* is a stamped impression of a prehistoric animal or plant found in rock.

Fossils of tiger bones found in Java and northern China show us the tiger first evolved over two million years ago. That means tigers, as a species, are really old!

Can you imagine being that old?

And that's not all the fossils show us. Fossils tell us that tigers were the first of the big cat family to evolve — even before lions, jaguars, and leopards! You may be thinking, "Yeah, yeah, I know tigers are old. I already know about the *sabretooth tiger*." We wouldn't blame you for thinking that. But actually, fossils and other evidence show us modern day tigers didn't descend from sabretooth tigers at all!

The sabretooth tigers all went extinct before the first ancestors of modern-day tigers ever came onto the scene. Modern day tigers come from an entirely different family tree that showed up much later. So now you know something about tigers that your parents and teachers probably don't know!

One more thing about tigers, from long ago. Did you know early tigers may have been ice skaters? Well, maybe they didn't exactly wear sparkly outfits and perform in the Olympics, *but they did walk across ice bridges once upon a time.*

Researchers believe that tigers were able to make their way into India through Northern Asia as a result of the last Ice Age. In India, the oldest tiger fossils were discovered inside the Kurnool Cave and were likely to be from the **Pleistocene Age** — which is a fancy way of saying a certain time period **long, long, looooong, ago!**

Snow leopard cubs

ARE TIGERS CLOSELY RELATED TO ANY OTHER ANIMALS?

Many scientists believe that tigers are closely related to other big cats like lions, jaguars, and leopards. However, it seems that tigers and snow leopards are more closely related than the rest, and this makes them the closest distant cousins!

By now, you're probably wondering just how similar tigers and cats are, right?

Well, here are the traits they share:

Cats and tigers have very similar body shapes – The tiger may be 60 times larger than a common cat. However, they both have strong but agile bodies, long tails that they use for balancing, narrow mouths and sharp teeth, as well as retractable nails!

They mark their territory in the same way – Both cats and tigers love to mark their territory, and they do this by spraying pee, rubbing their bottoms, and scratching objects. This is their way of saying, '*I live here, so back right off!*'

They prefer living alone – If you have a dog and a cat, you will have noticed that dogs need a lot more company than cats, overall. Cats are indeed quite solitary, just like tigers!

WHERE DO TIGERS LIVE?

A **habitat** is a location where an animal (or a person like you and me!) lives.

Tigers live in many habitats, such as forests, grasslands, and swamps. You know now that Siberian tigers love to live in cold places, but all other tigers prefer warmer climates. They particularly love rainforests!

So, where in the world are these habitats?

Scientists believe that about half of the remaining wild tigers in the world can be found in India. The remainder is spread throughout 13 countries – however, in some of these countries, there are very rare reports of wild tigers being spotted. So far, we know that India hosts about 3,000 wild tigers, while there are around 540 tigers in Russia, 400 in Indonesia, 360 in Malaysia, 230 in Nepal, and about 100 each in the tiny countries Bhutan, as well as Thailand.

WHY DO TIGERS HAVE STRIPES?

So they don't get SPOTTED!

CHARACTERISTICS AND APPEARANCE

As we now know, every tiger has distinct markings. These markings help the animal hide in the wild, especially at night when it is hunting prey.

While the six types of tigers share similar fur colors, there are a few differences that scientists have noticed. An example is the Sumatran tiger, which has darker orange fur than the rest of the tiger subspecies. It also looks darker because its stripes are much closer together.

Tigers living in colder climates will often have thicker fur than those living in warmer climates.

They even have some fur on their paws to protect them from the cold.

It's like having snow boots!

They usually also have another layer of fur around the neck (sometimes referred to as a scarf), which helps to further protect them from the cold. We are glad the tigers are well-dressed for playing in the snow, aren't you!

Another example of differences among the tiger groups is stripes on their legs. Some of the tiger groups have striped legs, but some do not.

FUN FACT: Did you know that if you shaved a tiger, it would still be striped? That's right. Tigers have stripes on their fur, but their skin is also striped. Although, we don't recommend trying to shave a tiger. We think it might get pretty mad!

WHAT UNIQUE FEATURES DO TIGERS HAVE THAT HELP THEM IN THE WILD?

Tigers are an amazing species, and even after years of research, we still don't know everything there is to know about them. However, we know a few things about their features and how these help a tiger throughout its life.

TIGER STRIPES

We already know that tigers use their colors as camouflage against the background to hide, but how do they do that? Their bright orange fur doesn't exactly seem like the kind of outfit you'd wear if you were trying to hide, right? You may not think a big orange cat with dark stripes is very good camouflage, but you aren't a prey animal.

Most of the animals that tigers hunt do not see the wide range of colors our eyes do. For animals with poor vision, it's hard to recognize the bold colors of a tiger as dangerous. Actually, they can't tell the contrasting orange color from the deep greens of long grass where the tiger is hiding, ready to pounce.

According to the experts at National Geographic, other animals see the tiger's stripes as moving shadows against the trees or the tall grass of their habitat. Pretty cool, huh!

TIGER SPOTS

Did you ever notice that tigers have white spots against black fur at the back of their ears? Scientists think these work as false eyes that could scare off other animals from committing a sneak attack behind them. Other researchers believe that these spots help their tiger cubs see their mom — even through the long grass!

TIGER TAIL

A tiger's tail measures as long as 3 feet! They use their tails to keep a steady balance even through the high-speed chases of hunting prey. Imagine how good your balance could be if you had a tail! This is also the reason your cat can balance on top of a tall fence or on a skinny ledge and not fall down.

TIGER CLAWS AND FEET

Tigers use their 4-inch claws to grab fast-running prey like deer. Their paws are also padded, allowing them to stalk or follow prey in complete silence. No clunky boots here! Tigers are barefoot hunters, but the pads are tough as the best leather shoes you own, making their feet hard but still great for sneaking up on a deer or wild boar.

At the same time, if you stretched a tiger's foot out and looked between their toes, you'd see a neat surprise! Each toe is connected with webbing (thin skin that goes between the toe). These webbed feet allow tigers to swim better and paddle their way through the water — kind of like when you put on flippers at the pool. This is especially handy if the tiger needs to travel through any water or cross a river when looking for its next meal.

HOW DO THESE CHARACTERISTICS HELP TIGERS?

Tigers are mostly **solitary** animals, which means they spend a lot of time alone and looking for food around their large habitats. According to experts, the tiger that keeps the biggest **territory** is the Siberian tiger. Territory is another word for their hunting ground. One Siberian tiger's territory in Russia covers over 4,000 square miles! That's about as big as the whole island of Hawaii, but with *far fewer pineapples*.

Pretty much the only time a tiger isn't alone is if she is a mother with cubs. The cubs will live with their mother until they are 1 ½ to 2 years old. Then they go off and find their own territory. There are also rare times when these big cats can be seen in a group, called an **ambush** — but this doesn't happen very often.

Tigers do their best to keep away from other predator animals, and they avoid conflicts with humans as best they can. However, tigers can still become aggressive, especially if they sense an invader inside their territory or feel threatened.

In the natural world, an adult tiger has very few predators. However, they can still be *harmed* by larger animals like buffaloes and elephants.

If a tiger can't avoid a fight, it will rely on its claws, teeth, and speed for its defense. But despite their power and ferocity, they are no match for humans with weapons.

As humans, we are the most dangerous threat to tigers because of the technology we have, such as guns. This is why so many tiger groups have been hunted to extinction and endangerment.

Thankfully, it is now illegal to hunt tigers, although sadly, poaching still exists.

HOW DOES A TIGER GREET OTHER ANIMALS?

Pleased to eat you!

WHAT DO TIGERS EAT?

Because tigers are carnivores, they hunt and eat big prey animals like wild boar, deer, and small elephants. They do this at night, and will generally avoid bigger, stronger animals. Because tigers also have a taste for cows, they often attack them with hopes of getting a tasty meal.

Once it kills its prey and eats as much as it can, the tiger will hide the rest of its meal from other animals and scavengers so that it can come back to finish it later. Tigers will also steal food from other big cats, such as leopards. This isn't nice, but it's all about survival in the big cat world, and getting a good meal is an important part of that.

A tiger's hunting skills are learned. No, tigers don't go to "tiger pre-school," though their mothers teach them everything they need to know. Mother tigers teach them how to hunt so that they can survive on their own and catch their own food as they grow older. Kinda like how adults also teach children how to hold a spoon, cut food with a knife and fork, and when they're older, how to cook for themselves!

Since tigers born in zoos never learn how to hunt properly, given they are fed by zookeepers, they can't return to the wild.

In their natural habitat, tigers have a lifespan between 10 to 15 years. When they become adults, they spend most of their life hunting and living alone. Inside a zoo, they can live up to around 20 years, and the oldest tiger ever recorded in a zoo became 25 years old. The record belongs to a Sumatran tiger named Djelita, who lived in the Honolulu Zoo.

WHAT DID THE TIGER SAY TO HER CUB ON HIS BIRTHDAY?

It's roar birthday!

TIGER CIRCLE OF LIFE
SIMPLE STEPS FROM CUB(BABY) TO ADULT TIGER

Breeding season for tigers usually happens between November and April, but they can also have babies at any time. A momma tiger will be pregnant with her babies for 100 days, and they usually have between 2-6 babies. Each cub weighs between 2-3 pounds at birth and is born totally blind, just like kittens! Since these babies are so vulnerable, mother tigers will try to find a safe place to give birth, such as inside a cave or in tall grass.

Because cubs are born blind, they rely on their mother for *everything*, including food and protection. A cub's eyes will open after 6 to 12 days. For the first 6 weeks of their life, they are cared for and nursed by their mom. The cubs are most vulnerable at this stage since they aren't strong enough to protect themselves.

When they turn 7 weeks old, cubs start to eat solid food provided by their mom, who will hunt prey and bring back meat to share with her babies. During this time, cubs spend most of their time chasing and wrestling with each other. This isn't all fun and games but also plays an important role as the young tigers grow. The cub rough-housing teaches them proper stalking techniques and strengthens their muscles.

At 8 weeks old, the cubs are ready to go out with their mom to watch and learn how to hunt. Between 8 to 10 months, cubs join their mom on her hunting trips. This is where they learn how to help bring food home — it's kind of like how you learn to go grocery shopping or how you cook with your parents!

Every litter will have a dominant cub who will be the leader during playtime and be more active than the other siblings. This cub will usually be the first to leave the family. Once they reach two years old, the other cubs will also move on to their own territories.

QUIRKY FACTS YOU PROBABLY DIDN'T KNOW ABOUT TIGERS!

Okay, you've learned a lot, but we bet you didn't know these unusual and fun facts about tigers!

TIGER PEE CAN SMELL LIKE BUTTERED POPCORN

The smell of buttered popcorn might sound delicious, but beware if you smell it when there's a tiger around! If you suddenly start smelling buttered popcorn in the wild (and you live in India or somewhere else where tigers live), you might want to turn around and head somewhere safe!

This is a sure-fire sign that a tiger has marked its territory!

TIGERS SWIM WITH THEIR HEADS ABOVE WATER

Remember how tigers are good swimmers because of their huge paws and webbed feet, but did you know they don't go all the way underwater?

Like many big cats, tigers hate getting water in their eyes. This is why they never let their head go underwater. As much as possible, tigers submerge themselves only up to their necks. If they really want to protect their eyes, they sometimes go into the water backwards.

Because they're good swimmers, tigers can cross rivers as wide as 18 miles. Aside from using it as a way to travel, tigers also swim to chase their prey into the water and trap them.

TIGERS USE THEIR SALIVA TO CLEAN THEIR WOUNDS

You might have seen pet cats licking themselves when they get hurt. Tigers do the same thing! They have what you call antiseptic saliva, or the type of saliva that cleans wounds. Since tigers don't have alcohol or Betadine to clean their injuries, they can use their saliva instead to help the wound heal and not get infected. Since there aren't tiger doctors they can visit if they get hurt, this is really important.

TIGERS CAN ROAR REALLY LOUD

Tigers don't just have big bodies — they also have big voices! In fact, their roar can be heard almost 2 miles away. To reach a distance of 2 miles, that would mean you would have to walk for 30 to 40 minutes. That's pretty far — and pretty loud!

Aside from having loud roars, tigers can also hiss, growl, grunt, moan, chuff, snarl, and gasp. Each sound is believed to have different meanings when they communicate with other tigers.

Can you speak tiger?

EASY TIGER!

DID YOU HAVE FUN LEARNING ABOUT TIGERS?

We hope you had a great time learning about these majestic animals! Tigers are now known to be "endangered" on the International Union for Conservation of Nature (IUCN) Red List. You might have encountered the word endangered a couple of times in this book already. It means almost all of the tigers are gone.

In the whole world, there are only about 4,000 tigers remaining in the wild. Even though it is against the law, people still hunt tigers for their fur and bones. There is an illegal market for tiger parts, which is really awful. Still, it's important you know it exists so you can ensure you and your loved one **never buy tiger products.**

If people around the world stopped buying tiger products, the poachers wouldn't have a reason to hunt them!

Tigers are also at risk of losing their natural habitats as people move in on the areas where tigers live. This forces tigers to live in areas closer to humans, which is not a good thing. Remember how tigers like being alone? They need to have space to hunt, and they need lots of prey animals to eat. If they live close to humans, they won't have these things. Conflicts can also happen because tigers are meant to be in the wild.

Even though very few tigers are left in the world, hard work, commitment, and love can help them bounce back from the brink of extinction. Together, we can all help these beautiful animals survive and, maybe one day, thrive again in the wild.

Just by learning about tigers and caring about them, you are helping to make that happen. Tell others how amazing tigers are and that they deserve our help!

Here are just a few simple ways you can help tigers survive in the wild:

- Make sure all the adults in your home **buy paper products that are FSC certified.** This means your toilet paper and paper napkins do not originate from fragile forests in Asia. In fact, why don't you also ask your school to ensure their products are FSC certified?
- **Avoid products containing palm oil** – this is also a product that is made from

forests all over Asia, many coming from habitats of tigers.
- For your next birthday, why not ask your parents to **adopt a tiger in your name**? Wouldn't that be cool?! You can ask them to adopt a tiger, on your behalf, from the World Wildlife Fund.

WHAT DO YOU CALL A TIGER THAT LIKES TO DIG IN THE SAND?

Sandy claws!

THANK YOU!

Thank you for reading this book and for allowing us to share our love for tigers with you!

If you've enjoyed this book, please let us know by leaving a rating and a brief review wherever you made your purchase! This helps us spread the word to other readers!

Thank you for your time, and have an awesome day!

For more information, please visit:

www.animalreads.com

HAVE A **ROAR-SOME** DAY!

© Copyright 2022 - All rights reserved Admore Publishing

ISBN: 978-3-96772-091-4

ISBN: 978-3-96772-092-1

Animal Reads at www.animalreads.com

The content contained within this book may not be reproduced, duplicated or transmitted without direct written permission from the author or the publisher.

Under no circumstances will any blame or legal responsibility be held against the publisher, or author, for any damages, reparation, or monetary loss due to the information contained within this book. Either directly or indirectly.

Published by Admore Publishing: Roßbachstraße, Berlin, Germany

www.admorepublishing.com

www.ingramcontent.com/pod-product-compliance
Lightning Source LLC
LaVergne TN
LVHW020140080526
838202LV00048B/3982